Toward the
Wild Abundance

For Irene, with best wishes

TOWARD THE WILD ABUNDANCE

Kristin Brace

POEMS BY ~~KRISTIN BRACE~~

WHEELBARROW BOOKS ▪ *East Lansing*

♾ The paper used in this publication meets the minimum requirements
of ANSI/NISO Z39.48-1992 (R 1997) (Permanence of Paper).

 Wheelbarrow Books
Michigan State University Press
East Lansing, Michigan 48823-5245

Printed and bound in the United States of America.

28 27 26 25 24 23 22 21 20 19   1 2 3 4 5 6 7 8 9 10

Library of Congress Control Number: 2018952540
ISBN 978-1-61186-322-2 (paper)
ISBN 978-1-60917-601-3 (PDF)
ISBN 978-1-62895-367-1 (ePub)
ISBN 978-1-62896-368-7 (Kindle)

Book design by Charlie Sharp, Sharp Des!gns, East Lansing, MI
Cover design by Erin Kirk New
Cover art: "New Day," original oil painting on canvas, courtesy
of Artist Jill Worm, represented by LaFontsee Galleries.

g green press Michigan State University Press is a member of the Green Press
INITIATIVE Initiative and is committed to developing and encouraging
ecologically responsible publishing practices. For more information about the
Green Press Initiative and the use of recycled paper in book publishing, please
visit *www.greenpressinitiative.org*.

Visit Michigan State University Press at *www.msupress.org*

With the publication of Kristin Brace's *Toward the Wild Abundance*, the Residential College in the Arts and Humanities (RCAH) Center for Poetry at Michigan State University offers its fourth book in our continuing project, the Wheelbarrow Books Poetry Series. Clearly, we pay homage to William Carlos Williams and his iconic poem, "The Red Wheelbarrow." Readers will remember that the poem begins, "so much depends upon" that red wheelbarrow. We believe that in the early decades of this twenty-first century, a time when technology, politics, and globalization are changing our lives at a pace we could hardly have imagined, so much does depend upon our determination to privilege the voices of our poets, new and old, and to make those voices available to a wide audience. So much depends upon providing a retreat, a place of stillness and contemplation, a place of safety and inspiration. So much depends upon our ability to have access to the words of others so that we see, regardless of race, religion, ethnicity, gender, economic situation, or geographical location, that we all share the human condition, that we are more alike than we are different. Poetry helps us do that. Edward Hirsch reminds us that poetry is one solitude speaking to another—across time, across space, across all our differences. Audre Lorde reminds us that poetry is not a luxury; it is a necessity. Walt Whitman knew that to have great poets, we must create great audiences. As our number of published books increases, we hope that our audience increases also. We hope to contribute toward the wild abundance of poetry in the world, words blossoming like wildflowers, lines like the webs of spiders connecting us at critical points, stanzas holding us like childhood cabins in the woods, places of safety and comfort, but also imagination and mystery. So much depends upon the collaboration of our readers and writers, the intimate ways they will come to know one another.

—ANITA SKEEN, *Wheelbarrow Books Series Editor*

remarked to a friend that over the course of my life I continue to be startled by the writer's imagination and the craft that allows a string of words to describe our lives anew. I stopped for a moment to consider the breadth of this sentiment. Why should I have stopped to reconsider the truth of this statement? Is it because I tired of my dependence on running, or because my passion for movies comes and goes, or because my wired world exhausted me enough to *not* connect to "friends" through social media? I love my family, but I don't want to be around them every day. My taste for food changes, as does my preference of wine. Is it a coincidence that I uttered these words the same day I chose *Toward the Wild Abundance* as the winner of the Wheelbarrow Books Prize for Poetry?

Toward the Wild Abundance by Kristin Brace conjures emotions initiated by the frailty and wonder of our lives. The multifaceted nature of this work demands that it be read for voice and validation. A second reading reveals a deeper commentary on the nature and value of art and the artist. These kaleidoscopic poems also shine brilliance on themes of memory and the passage of time. They fluidly transport us from past to present and into the imagination to pose questions about how our experiences inform identity and meaning.

"At the Café" is a great example. A woman sees a young woman she babysat—an ordinary occurrence. However, Brace uses extraordinary images and what seem like random connections to reflect on time passing. What limits or doesn't limit who we become? What would these women now say to each other?

Later in the poem, in the same café, two men have a seemingly innocuous exchange:

. . . "Hey, How are you?' Man two replies,
"Another day," which seems like "Same old, same old,"
but maybe he means, "Another day and I'm still

alive! The sun is shining, and look at this, this
miracle of structure and mobility: I'm walking!
And talking! At the same time!"

The final lines define sensuous longing in this moment:

The window boxes spill
petunias so lush, so sun-reaching and magnificent and
dark I want to eat them. That's what I want, right now:
pulpy, sticky, fibrous purple between my teeth.

Another provocative theme Kristin Brace explores is that of art itself and how we "see." In "Monologue of an Unknown Model," the silent voice of an artist's model projects her own version of blue from her corner—a vision we can *only see in our mind's eye,* validating that melancholy feeling we all have.

Or in "My Life As an Impressionist Painting," which begins with

Pay attention
to the light.

The way light is always expressed through color,
because even a magic paintbrush cannot drip with light.

If this poem stopped here, we would have enough. But the poem builds and builds into how art imitates life, or is it the other way around?

I'm honored and humbled to have chosen *Toward the Wild Abundance* by Kristin Brace for the Wheelbarrow Books Poetry Prize. Go to your chosen place and bask in this (or any) day's dose of her words.

—SARAH BAGBY

Contents

6. WHERE THE GRASS STILL GREENS

1.
Someone, Some Afternoon

Looking at Rooms Upside Down

Sometimes I do it when I flip
my hair over my head, twist

and coil the silky snake of it
into a bun. Sometimes I hang

my aching head over the edge
of the bed and all I see are stripes.

As a child, I wandered the house
with a hand mirror under

my chin, letting feet memories
guide me through rooms while

my mind walked the world
of the ceiling. How spacious,

that world, how free with its
air and light. The windows

stretched wider and every
inanimate thing felt curious.

Not to the touch, but rather
it seemed each object had

feelings, keen insight
into the absurdity of the world

as we know it, said this
is the world right side up,

welcome, you've found us out.
Better versions of all of us—

or a different us altogether—
must occupy those ceiling chairs,

their pillows staying put
through pure desire.

Sometimes a voice: Look out!
And I'd narrowly miss

the half wall breaking the family
room, feet scuffing carpet,

mind skating the blank
space above, now below.

Light glinted off the mirror.
In the flash, a disembodied

torso might appear, or wrong-
way arms, thumbs dumbly

frozen in a false thumbs up.
Plants were like wishes,

hovering just above the floor,
never getting too comfortable.

And I was nobody, nothing,
a face behind a mirror

in a made-up world, and that
made me magic, and real.

Dream to Start the New Administration

It begins, or possibly
ends, with the birds on the deck.
We gather around the table
at a childhood friend's
and there they are,
lined up in the snow,
looking in through the glass.

I have no doubt
the doors are locked.

Crow after crow in a tidy row,
waiting. Other birds, too,
like a giant stork that should
be white, but is black.
In every bird, not a speck of color,
black as charred wood, so black
the snow won't bounce back in gleam.
Not menacing, but expectant—
serene, yet easily startled.
I flinch at the glass
and a few birds hop back.
Others fly away. I wake and wonder

how well they could see
inside to the lighted table.
It was daylight, with snowlight,
and the light within was perhaps
not so bright, after all. Maybe
they were waiting, but all they saw
was their own reflection

dulling along with the hope
of ever getting in. Or maybe
they didn't want in at all,
but pitied us: bare palms pressed
to the table's manmade grain,
our high back chairs encircling
the electric bulbs' false glow.

Maybe, wary, they simply watched.
I had the feeling they knew
more than we did, that it had
something to do with patience.

Just Visiting

If time sanctifies,
     why do we not kneel in bashful
          reverence before trees?

And then, with knees still clean with
     dirt, stand palm to palm, gaze
    to gaze, and travel backward, sinking

inward to the place our
    baby animal spirits
       met   (cloudy eyes, pink tongues).

We have known each other

        forever. Remember

the yellow guest room, the damp sheets,
    where you held me and wrenched
       the jagged shard from my chest?
If time heals, why can't it just

hurry up?   (In the woods, a doe licks
             her fawn's wound to

stop its bleeding.)

That evening, we played dominoes, paving
    paths across the continent of the table. I wanted

to stand them on end like slippery
                tombstones, hold my breath, and tick
      the first with my fingernail, infant
            dictator's delight at the regimented
clatter.

The Year of the Cicada

The Year of the Cicada
        is also the Year of Abominable Health,
the Year of Body, Mind, & Soul Shipped
        to the Far Reaches of
                Nowhere, Somewhere, & Where.

It is the Year, too, of Silver & Gold,
        the Year of a Friend's Joy and a Friend's Departure.
The Year of the Most Movies
and a Continued Love Affair with
        a Wide Variety of Books.
The Year of Less Sex, More Sleep,
        of Almost Daily Popcorn with Butter,
of Giving Up and Trying Too Hard.

What is a year but a series of disappearing days?
A collection of Feeling Old and Feeling Young?

This year is the Year of Dreaming I:
        Ireland, Iceland, India, Italy,
        Identity morphed, the wet wings still.

Another year of no novel, no garden, no accordion.
A year of Closing the Cookbooks' Covers.
Maybe a year without a name, or a year called
        Reflections on a Grandmother's Beauty.

Requiem

All day I think of you,
as I tuck new sheets onto the bed,
fold towels and washcloths in neat
interlocking patterns on the kitchen table.
I trim the threads with scissors
the way you did, the seventh standing
figure in a family of six chairs.
One empty, and you were there
to fill the void, squeeze too much
honey into sick-day tea, hum
humming as you went about your work.
I set the timer to keep me accountable.
Rise when it rings, reach for the green
laundry basket propped by the door,
composing my lunch in my head:
leftover cabbage, corn tortilla with coarse
salt, pickled radishes, avocado sliced
just so. The slow dismantling
and the pleasure it brings.

Empty Boats

Make you think at first: catastrophe—
                              (the body's inner lunge)
the way the water is so still, as if someone
stopped splashing hours before. The way

the sun is brightness and nothing more,
the slick red leather of one seat giving
the light a grinning afterthought

of itself. The other boat abandoned further out,
the motor stilled. Somewhere—*sigh*—

men clamming. I was surprised
the first time I saw it, a man in no-color
waders, his shirt a brilliant flash of white
like a gull swooping close to the surface.
Different cut up shapes of him
through the bushes beyond the live oak.
I finally learned the name of that tree, a month
before we move away. The wind
has conversations with it regularly
and it won't miss us when we leave. Once

we saw our landlady moving
through the backyard's afternoon light
as in a dream. She wasn't wearing her wig
and her hair was sparse, wispy gray that barely
covered her head. She seemed lost

inside herself at river's edge. The wind

urges the water into sideways-turning fingers,
hands submerged, each curl clear when you see it
up close, but from here, only texture in the water.

If You Love It Enough

If you love it enough, anything will talk with you.

—George Washington Carver

We have our best ideas in childhood.
It's all downhill after that—or is it?
"Two turtles on a hill wearing hats,"
I wrote as a four-year-old, describing
my marker drawing on a tiny leaflet
of lined paper. Now we might say,
"Honey, let's make a GMO-free
baby together," or, "How about a dash
more cloves in the plum compote?"

At least there's still skinny-dipping.
Or fake skinny-dipping: taking
off your suit in broad daylight
once you're underwater,
a stone's throw from shore.
How that teensy bit of fabric
keeps you tethered. You can
keep the shore to your back

and play a harmonica in your mind,
envision shipwrecks and fresh
water salmon and vast schools of
slick minnows and midsummer
in Sweden a few hundred years ago.
What kind of flowers would you
wear in your hair? Something

plucky for me. Little balloons of
heady scent, hardy enough to twine
with ribbons, flowers with a
funny provincial name like
hog's foot or sheep's teat that
die in a day. Something pink.

Bonnard

Someone cut the nudes right out of the book.
It wasn't an act of censorship—no, *Nude in the
Bathroom* was snipped while *Nude in Lamplight*

remains. Which means—what else?—a patron
of the public library has a thing for the nudes with

Coverlet and *Toque*. And who wouldn't?
Nudes are all the nuder with tilted hats and shawls
adorning their figures, reminding admiring
viewers of their nudity, *n'est-ce pas*?

The author's description of *The Bath*
complements a painting with white railing, vague
persons gazing beyond a choppy sea

to a lilac and blood orange horizon. Confusion
first arises with *Nude Against the Light.*

The title is paired with a hazy woman
wearing white, open book on her lap, tea
forgotten, her attention drawn to a black cat
poised in the olive green shadows of the lawn.

A quarter inch of page between mismatched
image and text—easy to miss if not
brushed by the inner wrist—betrays the act.

Was it with scissors? A penknife? Committed
at the library, or at home? Where, now,

does Bonnard's "very personal vision of the
female nude" reside? On a bulletin board,
perhaps. Or in a manila folder, filed under
Art, Bonnard, Nudes. Maybe they're framed

and hung on a papered wall, nudes of all make
and model intermingling with magnolias,
blossoming from gold and umber branches,

sumptuous and uncouth. Someone,
some afternoon, will visit the nude-lover's home.

A heavy curtain will be tugged to one side
and the sun will spill diagonally across the wall,
as if a mountain, out of sight, kept
from the magnolias that triangle of light.

The visitor's eyes will fall on a series of prints
illuminated behind dusty glass. The host will remark
casually on the dreamlike quality of Bonnard's work,

how it casts a spell: you can turn your gaze away
and swear you hear his leaves rustling, look down

to see your arms dappled with their light.
Close your eyes, the host will say. Listen to the drip
of bathwater as hand reaches to neck, submerges,
raises dripping fingers to pink-tinted brow.

The host will grow impassioned, begging
notice of the lavender shading on the bather's
flesh like the quiet of winter shadows on snowy fields.

A clock will tick. A stranger's radio will play softly
the other side of the wall. Something timeless,

perhaps a French musette, something in a minor key.
The visitor will shift a little, suddenly
eager to leave and knowing it is too soon,
becoming aware of every joint rigid inside their clothes

and the faint musty smell of the carpet.
The host will fiddle with some trinket, something silver
and slim from another era and say, "I knew a girl

who saw the bare backs of people's arms in coffee shops
and had to keep herself from kissing them."

A Pomegranate, or a Rhyming Couplet

Anything that fits
        in a picnic basket,
really. A chilled bottle and
        napkins, pressed. Oh,

you would say
        I'm doing nothing.
Or, something:
        wasting time.

What if I told you
        I walked
in the woods with
        William Stafford,

that I floated on a
        snowflake, held a
moment of grief called
        The Modern World

Stops Singing? I
        can't promise you
clean dishes or even
        a story concluded.

But my third eye
        is an entire
blue-green world.
        And this tablecloth

is a garden where I
        could lose myself

and maybe find
        us, an easy breath,

succulent fruit. Put down
        your shoulders
and your rustling fears.
        Take, eat.

2.

That Pale Blue Space

Headache

I am unable to distinguish
between the feeling I have for life
and my way of expressing it.
                              —Henri Matisse

I would paint it if I could:
skull a wooden frame brushed
yellow as canaries, tight and
tacky in the humid air.
Earthen heft of glazed
clay pressed into forehead,
cinched with steel over bridge of nose,
emblem of the lake
that weather and illness
keep separate from me.
And here, welded to the bone-weary
tip of first vertebra wobbles
an electrical box, charged
by lawnmower-drone and weed-
wacker-buzz, each surge
of caustic voltage building
pressure in this lemon-
squeezing brain. Copper
poorly wired, electrons
misfired—like the brown out

back home that sepia-toned
the whole cul-de-sac.
Mom called the ornery
neighbor to ask what was
going on and for just a moment,
we were allies, observing

together as a mad, invisible
artist hand-tinted the
atmosphere pink, then yellow,
then green. "The end
of the world," I thought by my
bedroom window. But
so many things were yet to be:

yet here my mind pulls
a cord and down drops a
gauzy white curtain, as if
so much could claim that space
yet to be
that every memory shies
from filling it. All I see is
something like what I feel
in the back of my head:

all of us grown,
and the side door to the garage
still not hooked in place the way
Mom wanted. Warm garage air
on one side, smelling of gasoline,
carpet, and potting soil;
on the other, a fresh
breeze blown past the dead
crab apple and the dying maple
where my brothers once perched
the family cat. Everyone
gone and the white painted door
with its pollen dusted windows
left swinging.

Monologue of an Unknown Model

It seems the Swedish girl is not happy; her Jules has
vanished and I am going to try to find another model.
—From a letter by Mary Cassatt
to Berthe Morisot, autumn 1879

Well I know
something of the color blue. I see
it rise from the earth each morning,
in dense, damp wonder drawn
from slumber by the sun until, startled,
it finds its stillness among ferns
and moss in the wood.

Everyone knows the blue of a daytime sky. But I
see the wistful blue of a girl not given
silk ribbons to tie up her yellow hair.
The blue of broken crockery whose insides
are brown and common as the earth.
The blue of chicory dusty on the roadside
that wilts and dies the minute you uproot it.
I know the blue of a house collecting shadows.
I know the blue at the bottom
of a white porcelain pitcher. Pine trees
clutching blue to their dark undersides, sending
vast coils of wanting upward in search of stars.
I know the blue of wishing.

Blue of a lamb born too soon.
Blue of hydrangeas, a forgotten
afternoon. Blue called absence and empty.
Behind my eyes, the inky blue night sky

and the earth a snarl of worsted wool
in heaven's shearling black,
the ocean's froth and someone's silence
just gleaming shards of bone.

I know the blue pinwheels sewn
into the quilt of the bed I may never
share. Rivers in the tender underside
of my arm: snow white, he said,
but what did he know? He never
brushed at dusk in the corners of a room,
sweeping and sweeping at the blue
that gathers there like blue between two stones.

Re-creationism

On the second day,
fog congregated in the low places
and the not so low,
everywhere last year's
stiff cattails stood startled
and the rain-wet trees
bled sap and almost-green.
But it was January,
and the robins needn't come
when the deer's lashes still
flick in intuitive fear of hunger.
You could see inside
the bare twigs glistening
and rich with rain. You could
hear them growing
in their sleep.

The Names of Things

When her ovaries hurt she imagines them
as full, heavy roses, deep pink, drooping
in the bruise of dusk. (Unborn children's names
escape in curling tendrils of green or as
final sighs loosed in faint floral breath.)
Or maybe they are a head of purple cabbage,
lobotomized, drying in the sun. There: a gray
squirrel in the curly willow salvages a seed.
Bodiless legs between low pine boughs cross
in a pale X. In the gathered murmur of adoring
leaves, two magnolia blossoms fill with light.

Here, a hat on the wall. A dog asleep in the sun.
In her mind, her body moves: hand grasps
the enameled watering can, foot passes St. Fiacre
on the step. The gardener that lives here says
he is only an outdoor flower arranger. She calls herself
old-young, motionless wanderer, wanter
and not wanting. Touching each darkness
inside her with the finger of her mind,
she sets them thrumming until they glow with color:
periwinkle, citron, cat's tongue pink.
She calls them by names even she cannot speak.

Somewhere in Newfoundland

swims a body of water
marked Disappointment Lake.
It could be

that it's unimpressive,
but I'd like to think it was named
for holding lost hopes, for welcoming
wanderers who carry broken dreams

like stones in their hands.
It's a lovely lake, really, with mist slinking in

like a prodigal cat each morning,
creeping over the surface and resting
its head on the pine-soft shore.

It's a good lake, with reeds
and lily pads, and frogs for the lily pads,
and happy fish, and turtles lined up
sunning on blackened logs.

Wind riffles the surface and loons
tune the air tremulous with their song.

Silence flocks in from miles around.
And with it, the weary come.
Feet find cool water without compass or map.

All are certain of their purpose here.
Among the travelers
stand my mother—on a broad stretch
where the lake breathes and you

feel at home in its lungs—and there,
my father, who crouches now near an inlet,

thinking like a fish. Neither is aware
that the other is here.
My mother wears her patterned shirt

that always smelled of her: an old perfume
you can no longer buy and a mixture
of apricots and irritation, laughter,
and hay sweetened by the sun.

She holds in her palm
the baby teeth of all her children,

plucked from the top left bureau drawer
where they've hidden for years in tiny boxes.
Now, all the teeth are jumbled together,

molars rounded down by words for her ear,
canines that slid into strawberries and
nipped at flesh. They represent things with
capital letters: Forgetfulness, Longing, the Secrets

she was made to keep. My father, in another crook
of the lake's body, wears a red plaid shirt

and glasses from two decades ago.
He's holding a time-thin drawing
of a smiling girl in a purple dress

with a giant bow in her hair. He's holding
a stack of business cards from jobs
he never liked. My mother tosses
the teeth in an arc and they join the water

like fat drops of rain.
They sink slowly, drifting

among soft plants and decaying fish,
until they settle in the sandy
bottom to become fossils my father

would like to find. My father tries
to scatter his papers but the wind
is wrong and they flap back to brush
his body and fall to the water's surface.

So he picks them up
and wades with them into waist-high water,

the depth of a father in Lake Michigan
teaching a daughter not to be afraid.
He holds the papers under until

they grow pulpy in his fingers.
The water thrums around him like
a sleeper's pulse. He raises his face
and sees what my mother, unseen, has

already seen: a kingfisher, watching.

It's happening again so I'm writing

sunny Sunday sunny Sunday sunny—
sun and I'm cold in my holey
sweater in my plaid in my stripes in my
fox feet, writing for the quail on the
chipped English cup writing
for the out-of-tune piano for the fallen
strand of purple vine for every
woman poet who hasn't yet been named
editor of *The Best American Poetry*
for all the journals who send
such nice rejection notes and then reject
the next piece I offer. Writing

for the pebbles, silky white
in memory and moonlight,
sifting underfoot at the house
that was yours. For sneaking just now
to the back of the house when my
husband came home—for my husband
and for the sneaking. For the scent
of oil pastels and the foot-feel of a
woven rug. For Claire in Montana
and Claire around the corner.
For the spider plants, dying.
For everything and everyone
that is dying. For the great green
heart at the center of the earth,
full of sorrow-joy, full of
longing, dripping with remembered
light as if with butter, like the Kerry

Gold at my aunt's in San Francisco
where we spent my thirtieth, and I
thought how sad we know each other
so little, this aunt who stands like me
and walks like me and waves her hands
like me—or I like her—the way
we both say yeah, yeah. How you
can miss and love and imagine
that she misses and loves and how
it's that wondering in between
where everything happens,
that pale blue space
that makes all the difference.

William Stafford and George Eliot: A Conversation

WS: Sometimes commanders
take us over, and they try to
impose their whole universe

GE: She is *not* my daughter,
and I don't feel called upon
to interfere

WS: No task I do today
has justice at the end.
All I know is

        —hemlock, spruce, then shore pine—

GE: On the contrary, I think
it would be wicked of me
to marry you even if I did
love you.

WS: Lost you. What happened
to Ella? Where does she live?

GE: She had woven a little future,
of which something like this scene
was the necessary beginning.

        as absurd as a faith that believed
in half a miracle for want of strength
to believe in a whole one.

WS: Strange how things in the world
go together even when you don't try.

GE: So she went on in her neutral tone,
            as if she had been remarking
            on baby's robes

            . . . conceive the effect
            of the sudden revelation

WS: And you can't have that
            soft look when you pass.

Sunday in the New House

When the talk turns to cancer and dying,
it is the deer that soothe me, unaware and
uncaring, stepping through the field across the road.
New leaves soften the slope of their necks.
Ears twitch, eyelashes brush coarse fur,
velvety noses and long tongues dip
low to the teeming earth. This side of the window I see
how they carry their stillness with them.

When I Hear a Gentle Knocking

This is what I think, in this order, in the space of a second:

It's you, with something delicious to tell me, not wanting
to disturb me, but too excited not to, feet cold on the tile,
ear tilted in listening, expectant and dimpled and sweet.

Early teens, in the shower at Dad's apartment, growing
irate while shampooing as someone pounds on the door,
locked against trespass to my windowless sanctuary,
someone bent on driving me insane. Then my dad's voice
over the spray of water and my intermittent screams
at "whoever it is" to shut up: "It's Daddy, honey, I'm just
fixing the other door." My "oh" engulfed in the steam
and my wonder at his gentleness.

The ghost of a woman who lived here once.
She wears a silver bun and black starched apron,
and being born over a century ago,
she is polite enough to knock.

Migraine Hates Turbulent Change

from A Brain Wider Than the Sky *by Andrew Levy*

Migraine wears pinstripe trousers
while traveling

Migraine adores massive fireplaces found
in great English halls, surrounded by tapestries
and people with faces ruddy from the hunt—

but thinks, "odious, squabble-swamp,
thunk" if offered hot buttered rum

Migraine feels pale yellow
while peering from windows on trains

Migraine is a puddle and the boots
when it rains

Migraine still reads real newspapers,
relishes the pages' crisp flip

Migraine might be Episcopalian

Migraine prefers pottery with a smooth
glaze, but only if it's something you can
lift with two hands

Migraine has no hands

Migraine likes evergreen, violet, umber—

unless there's a lightning storm, then it's
indigo, terracotta, electric
lemon, dove and charcoal, neon pink

Migraine hates politics, flat pillows,
and poems of which it's the subject

Migraine can cut paper snowflakes
for hours

Migraine appreciates citrus, but not
when the moon is full

Migraine is smarter than you, even
though it doesn't have a brain

Migraine won't take vitamins or keep
a calendar

Migraine is probably not really Episcopalian,
but likes the velour cushions dented
by communicants' knees

Migraine doesn't have knees

But Migraine has a thing for well-
turned ankles (and probably Victorian
soft pornography)

Migraine may come with the changing
wind, but never really left

Don't put Migraine in a mint green box
with a tight plastic slot for a label

Don't put Migraine in a hammock
or on a high-speed ferry

Don't give Migraine black pepper,
sweet wine, or a lighter

Don't light a candle for Migraine

Migraine is here to stay

Outside the Frame

The world in turmoil and I remember
a voice, dissatisfied (dis-
appointed, other words that start with *dis*).
Rationality is a concept and therefore
can't quite fight off the draping
of expectation's thick cloak.
It hovers above my shoulders.
Make it luxuriant, then, make it
impractical white. Make it mink
(but faux, as I have no need of furs).
Most of all, just make it go away. Or make it
a Cassatt, all pinks and peaches and bath time,
bond of pure necessity and desire.
Make the whole world turn on the gentle
cleansing of a small, plump foot.

3.
Everything Familiar and Strange

Intuitively Meaningful Units of Lost Days

Migraine Disability Assessment (MIDAS) scoring measure

Matisse flourished his pinking shears
and raised a square of damask to the light:
brandied cherries, or claret? (Either
would be nice.) No. Not right.

He adjusted his spectacles and swished
a cerulean charmeuse from the shelf, let it
rise in the air with a flick of his wrist
and settle on the wide wood table.

He asked what Mary Ruefle would write
scores of years later: "Should a portion
of God's honest work be wasted?"
Fronds of philodendron bowed in contemplation

and Henri's scissors went snip, snip, snip
and the world's oceans slipped to the floor.
At the parting of the veil, a young canary
singing golden in its cage heard an old bird's voice

in its head: "Ah, yes. The necessary
sequester." The bars glinted in the sensual
touch of a sun burning nearly 93 million miles away,
the same sun that would hide

one day from a head whose eyes would read
a quick window burst upon the computer screen:
"Your keyboard is divorceable." And the head,
connected to a poet's heart, would cause

the body to throw its arms in the air and cry,
"Is everything divorceable now?"
And tectonic plates shifted and
another floe of iceberg drifted

out to sea. Oh Polar Bear, be careful
where you tread. At the zoo,
the polar bear tossed a chunk of bone
in the air and leaped after it—

paws spread, surge of water,
children's laughter and the poet's
giggle. She surprised a man with that non-
adult sound. In the second story,

she does too much thinking: What is the
True first story, and will there be a last?
Not long ago, lying awake after
her husband fell asleep, she heard

a mouse sneeze in the kitchen.
It was preposterous, storybook and
sublime and she felt indignant,
she had to wake him. He would not

be roused. So she lay looking into the dark
and said these words to herself:
"A mouse sneezed in the kitchen
and the day was lost."

Bathmat

Sometimes I wonder why we keep it.
Faded, frayed, once-purple-blue.
But not that. The master
bath, the time before, my sister
and I maybe eight and five.
The way it wasn't tucked flush
to the door when she showered,
how it might allow water to seep.
He chastised her for that non-fault,
that gap of tile, that thin cold line
and my sister said, "Mom did it."

To her the lie was a paper crane,
pure and crisp and white, nimble to fly
through the light-filled window.
But I added his finger, his hunch,
his "She did it wrong,"
and swallowed that crane, instead.
In my belly, it unfolded.
The paper wasn't white at all but
thick and fibrous, inked
with the words rift, shatter, tear.

Wide Awake Not-Nursery-Rhymes

Mama gave birth to a blackbird   (blackbird)
Mama gave birth to a crow   (shh)
Mama grew wings like an apron
Took a moon trail over the snow

Green sky blue sky green sky blue
Buckle my sweater, button my shoe
Blue sky gold sky gray sky red
Tuck in my trousers over my head

Meet me in the middle of somewhere, nowhere
Meet me in the middle of the rain
Meet me in the middle of a novel, would you?
Meet me in the whistle of a train

Sleep threw a penny in the pig pen   (what?)
Sheep took a dollar to the bank
The piggy bank sank in the pig sty   (big sigh)
Money money always stank

The pillow full of feathers flew to Amsterdam
The moon booked a cruise on the river
The sun was a ruby in a crown of pines
And the pigeon had a parcel to deliver

At the Café

Behind the espresso machine, a pair of long-lashed
brown eyes I recognize—a girl I babysat over
fifteen years ago. A sort of reluctance in her tanned
features, the dip of her head. I don't say anything—
not now—but images come back: the sunroom
with flat green carpet strewn with toys. How I was
grossed out and impatient when, as a toddler,
she needed help on the toilet and I was too rough.
How I saw the startled look in her eyes and felt
terrible from that moment onward. And now I feel sad
and awkward seeing those same eyes over the
cup of double espresso, like I know some weighty and

personal thing that grows heavier and more intrusive,
more real, as I sit outside under a black patio umbrella:
like a rag soaking up water from a bucket, staying wet
and clumped even when the rest of the water evaporates.
Maybe it has to do with what I know came later, what
I've wondered about certain years of her growing up.
A woman stoops for my dropped pen and continues
down the sidewalk, two young girls in tow—the last
and littlest with a swish of shiny-dark hair and scuffed,
black leather boots. A girl who knows what she wants.
A woman on the patio looks like a girl I met studying abroad.
Her parents were from England and she said her *th*s
almost like *f*s. People thought she had an impediment.
I wondered if she tried to unlearn it, the way I eased out of
certain Wisconsin vowels learned and normal as a kid.

At the top of the page, I almost predate the day
by an entire year. The sidewalk succumbs to coleus maroon
and chartreuse. From one side of the cafe's sandwich

board stretch a dog's toffee-colored back legs. Black, sun-
drenched paws poke out on the other. The girl who used to be
three brings my avocado toast with chili flakes and lemon.
We smile and talk and it feels more normal.
The mom and girls pass by again, facing me this time.
The youngest, shuffle-stomping, still brings up the rear.
Too-large glasses perch on her nose and she stares at me
through smudged lenses. What does she see? I doubt
she thinks of the future, sees only a stranger with a pen.

A man calls from his table to another man crossing
the street, "Hey, how are you?" Man Two replies,
"Another day," which seems like "Same old, same old,"
but maybe he means, "Another day and I'm still
alive! The sun is shining, and look at this, this
miracle of structure and mobility: I'm walking!
And talking! At the same time!" The dog and its people
are gone. A cluster of blonde-haired siblings
flocks to the open table. The tallest boy wanders away
to climb a tree. The oldest sister, braids
down her back, perches the youngest on her hip.
So familiar, that gesture of rag-tag motherliness,
the tidy hair. We're all spread out now, pins in a map:
West, Midwest, East Coast. Two cats gone and

one wiry vagabond remaining. I've arrived late
morning, having left St. Francis and Matisse at home—
my childhood home, my mother's. I'm house sitting,
everything familiar and strange. I'd stuffed my books and
pens in a bag I found in her closet, a real fish stamped
on the canvas in red below my youngest brother's name in
precise, pool-colored puffy paint. I'm trying to read a book

on the American purity movement. The window boxes spill
petunias so lush, so sun-reaching and magnificent and
dark I want to eat them. That's what I want, right now:
pulpy, sticky, fibrous purple between my teeth.

To Do

Brush hair like Rapunzel
(don't let suitors climb it)

Consider wall hanging
with embroidered hair:
technique, design, whose

Find lotion that turns
pointer finger back into
pointer finger from
frightening, helmet-
headed baby manatee
(much as you'd love
a baby manatee)

Draw a window
Open it

Draw a house
Build it

Have a frank conversation
about babies (don't
name babies Frank)

Practice qigong
Practice Italian
Practice the art of holding still
Breathe

Breathe

Do birthday cartwheels
on the beach
until you can't
(then remember
how they called you
Cartwheel Queen)

Swim in the light
of long-dead stars

Dream once more of whales

Verb 333

Today we are learning the eleventh form,
Future Perfect, of the verb *preferire*.
Say with me, *"Avrò preferito."*

I will have preferred. In this perfect future,
I'll have preferred heavy paperback books
to hardcover any day, and a desk

strewn with color so when crayons
and pastels are swept aside, they create
a new language every time. I'll

have preferred the unexpected weather,
the less-than-perfect dinner, the exquisite
bottle of wine. I'll have preferred

tombstones and train yards to nightclubs
and anyplace that eschews classic novels,
or accordions, or the lower vegetables

(such as celery, sort of the scullery maid
of vegetables—the sturdy, dependable
stalk that isn't noticed till it's gone).

The Future Perfect is Mediterranean
warm and Lake Michigan in winter.
It's paws curled close in kitten sleep.

It's admitting being wrong
instead of always being right.
It's more "we tried" and less "we wish

we had." *Avrò preferito una vita*
in which we still believe that anything
is possible, that oppression of the voiceless

can be lifted like a midsummer storm,
that the purest form of extravagance
is melting butter in a pan, singing.

Body of Work

Something serious comes to mind:
collected contributions to mineralogy,
theology, literature of the highest brow.
Probably a body made by a body
with a bushy, white mustache.
A body of work revered in hushed tones,
the creator's name rolling from tongues
golden and compact, gilding the phrase
                            the fruit of thine labor.
          Ah—

but here is a body of work most nimble.
          Back-strapped baby,
sweat blooming under straps, bucket snug in front, plunk
of cherries. Quick fingers in the leaves
          dusty and rustling. And her mind, a spreading
canopy of synapses entwined, linking
languages native and new, branching
          back to other orchards, faces
she no longer sees. Baby stretches,
          bucket fills. And I at my desk

writing and ready for distraction
picture the bowl of cherries chilling in the fridge.
          Market fresh, plump with summer light.
Fruit that, later, will become
a part of me—
          fructose, phosphorus, manganese
dissolving on tongue, traveling in darkness,
igniting mitochondria.
          This body that is work to nourish
          and clean, strengthen and maintain.

Body of mysterious pains and longings,
        body that falters and disobeys. Body
that houses the heart which knows
much more than I ever will understand.

My body of work will not be this flesh
nor these words on a page,
        but the light bending low through the window
to illuminate everything.
                Not the surety
of printed word nor solidity of bone, but the fleeting
memory of moonlight slung across a river, of a narrow
        street in a town on the other side of the world,
of a robin singing in praise or hope of rain.

My body will meet your body
        when I enter the kitchen full of cherry-thoughts,
gutters full of leftover rain.
Lips press lips, words from mouths
                wander to ears, O bodies
that won't always be, O lives that won't always
        be remembered.
                You'll have washed
your shirts, bought new for a new line of work,
        and hung them to dry. White,
button-down, no iron needed, damp and waiting
                        in the dining room. They swing
        from window molding and knobs.
Two like faded sphinxes flank our bedroom door.
        My mind counts one more, out of sight:
around the corner by the purple desk, the final shirt
        sways at the northern window
                full of air and light.

Sometimes, pink clematis climbing

a pocked power line pole is enough
to make me cry. I did cry when they cut down
the maple bordering our rental property
and the neighbors' back yard.
Eight AM and the sawing and
grinding of tree flesh, the apocalyptic
crunch and thud of machinery. Trucks
rumbling up and down the drive.
I showered, packed a lunch behind
closed blinds. Fled
through the front door and didn't

look back. After work,
I crouched by the carnage and
counted rings. Scent of gasoline
and sawdust ripe in the trampled dirt.
The cross-section was scarred by the saw
and I had to jump from decade to
decade in search of something legible.
One hundred years old. Once-
hidden houses gape. One hundred years old.
Forget learning from leaves as from books,
read: euthanasia for trees.

And what of the cardinal pair
that nested there in its branches?
The tottering baby skunks whose mother
lay flattened on the street,
that waddled and chirped at the hearth
of the maple's mellow heart when they tired
of eating ants between parked cars? Ours
is a privileged existence.

One hundred years of hush, one hundred
years of no harm, one hundred years
here growing and giving its living shade.
A century of solace, gone,
in the unthinking clatter of a Thursday morning.

Now I see sky where once I thrummed
in the mad green quiet of photosynthesis.
Always giving of itself, the sky unrolls
the thunder that smooths my face,
lends me shards of lighting
when I have no words.

Portrait of Valentine Godé-Darel
by Ferdinand Hodler (1914)

Speed Art Museum, Louisville, Kentucky

The eyes must say it all.
No longer filled with fear or agony
but a weariness so deep
I cannot make their brown
brown enough. Their lids become wedges:
the earth in the sun's orange light
or crescents of the sweet fruit dripping
from our fingers last Christmas morning.

Bruises rise to the surface of your cheeks
and I paint them like ice floes
bound in the cracked leather satchel of your skin. Quick—
in unmixed strokes, blue
of water that restores, to dash
about your shoulders like a cloak.

Behind you, a sky that waits for snow.
How softly it used to fall outside our window.
The room was quiet, sun on ice
flashing beyond the panes. Your perfect lobes
question marks curving from your hair.
My lips remember their tender flesh and I am afraid
that by painting them, I make your silence permanent.

So I paint a country road across your clavicle,
a town inside the hollow of your throat,
where once I saw a drop of water quiver

like the heartbeat of a sparrow. Your jawline
blurs, the effect of light shimmering on the horizon.
Everywhere, I paint you green: green
like unripe fruit, or moss that clings to stone.

Squander

Gassie: name of the lowly marble,
my favorite, gleaned in the frenzy
of gravel and fingers on the baseball
diamond of Pine Ridge Elementary.
Named, perhaps, for the rainbowed
puddles of oil in gas station lots. But spills
are everywhere—so who knows? Fever folds
these bright bits of memory hot

then cold into my pulse, *pulse, pulse.*
Forehead: a gray slab crushed
by cars driving by outside. Inside
my ears, birds chirp and feed
their young. I lie on the floor four
days sick and think of those who are
four weeks sick, four months
sick, four years or decades sick, peoples
and towns head sick, belly sick, heart
sick for centuries. And the unfairness

is loose pebbles skittering
in the back of a rickety pickup.
And my mind says: road trip, back
road. Star-fish-first-star. Peonies
tossing their heads in glorious self-
destruction, cabbage heads with
wax like milk, tigers padding through
moonlit snow, paddles slipping, silent,
through salt water, the deep
water behind my eyelids

where my vision sinks like stones.
Face up on the black futon
mattress, I float in the center
of the room. Up above hangs
the unlit ceiling light, flat
and round as a storybook moon.
On the small, gold circle
at its center is painted a miniature
icon of me, motionless, mattress-bound.

I am shrouded in pattern of
jungle leaves, bright colors to burst
into brighter flames, my bier moments
from being released into the eternal river.
How I wish, then, as the books
filling this room turn weightless,
(before I become ordinary dust

marring the water with my memory)
that they would abandon the book shelves,
end tables, and radiators to float
like luminaries beside me, offering comfort
with their sideways wisdom and their sorrows.

Lukewarm Coffee at a Blue Desk in Michigan

Words curdle. Words evaporate.

Words reconstitute in the scent of strong coffee,

        in the kicked-up odor of wet, decaying leaves
    present even in summer outside these city walls.

Our words were never

    our
        words.

The hand
        can take up a pen or a brush
and create symbols: flesh
        pulling meaning from nothing.

And how full that nothing is
        with the dust motes in the church where you painted,

        with the light of guttering votives
            circling the Virgin's skirt.

Full with silent prayers and the cold breath
        of cobblestones. I often wondered

where you walked: satchel slung over shoulder,
           shirt scrunched down to the skin of you,
        the little current of air you generated—if it were
visible—a deep blue-green.

The eyes of my heart would follow you

up hills and down,
                    through the cool
           shadows of grocery, garden, and nave,

through the sun's stream beamed back
               from walls, beneficent.

I rested my forehead
               on your train window to Rome.

I followed you to the seashore
               where you grew strong on wind and light.
               I followed you not knowing
where you lived till I left for good.

To think my fingers could have touched that door.
To think my palm could have pressed the cool metal, turned;
               that I could have entered and known.

My hands kept busy with bread
                    and cup, with glass and guidebook,
           each day cradled
by the guttural beauty of the cool air at night.

(For the night had an imperceptible sound—
               a dark, creaturely groaning and a

                    lilt soft as wings in cypress trees—
which unfurled

               something like waking in the womb.)

Triptych of Saints and Mistakes

I.   Who left the door ajar?
             Who tilted the room to let the light spill so?

             The ferns in the glade are humming.
             The trees are swaying their listening fingers
             and keeping their stillness alive.

             Brook, singing gladness in the shade.

II.   Here, at the bend in the road,
                 I planted a stone.

             A sign read this way or
                    that way and I sat down
             to watch the sun boiling red in the field.

III.   Remonstrance is a shabby word.
             Let us befriend curlicue,
                  rumple, and sludge.
             Let us gather great fistfuls
             of dirt to our ears and listen.
             Let our toes commune with the worms.

Fragments

I dreamed I met a woman in green
who, I thought, was what she told me—
but maybe we were part of the same.
She handed me a page and there
I read my name at the beginning of
a proper Latin name and the pictures
and the words drew the veil away.
I knew myself for what I was:
the closest human relative to the bird.

*

The word processor eats my name
and offers instead

contradistinction

buckminsterfullerene C_{60} (~soccerball)

a "super-duper benzene ring"

electroencephalogram

*

I am sitting on a king sized bed,
dark spread rumpled on my crossed legs,
sorting through postcards to aid
in my escape. Each picture contains
a different message for others on the run
and for those who are left behind.

*

Jenny in a yellow dress,
old-fashioned floral.
Dinner is late in the old family

kitchen, but she regrets she can
no longer help with preparation.
She's broken a nail down deep to its
half-moon bed.

*

I woke up in that smoke-blue cabin
with my guardian fox-dog warming
the small of my back with its paws.
I woke up there, and I can't remember
which happened first: I felt
your presence beside me, or I was content.
The window was moon-washed, the pine trees were
moon-washed. A barred owl called, unseen.

*

An old admirer's surprise
kiss on my right shoulder

Cowering under rickety
stairs while a recording shakes
the room: Nazis goose-stepping
and the Luftwaffe's drone

A dead snake
that turns out to be alive

*

A small bird catches an insect,
both in flight, a bright sun.
So close I see the light move

through the insect's green body.
And the bird's dark round eye
looking back at the world
shows me how little I truly know.

4.
You Might Be Yourself

Origin

The child was occupied with a scab all afternoon.
He wanted to ask his mother the meaning of
katydid, but she was walking a tightrope between
Guilt and No Regret. It looked a lot like
starting the dishes, looking down at the phone
in her hand, trimming the ends of the dahlias
again. In another century, a woman thumps
dough on the counter and the spume of flour
makes her think of a chickadee in the snow,
pulse like tidy stitches, the wings' quick flutter.
She'd always wanted to see a great horned owl.
Great Horned Owl, in all capitals like something
whispered from a storybook. Willow. Shortcake.
Evenings, she cross-stitches the origins of things.
Cassiopeia. Joan of Arc. Every small sacrifice.
Summer keeps her company on the sill.
Honeysuckle. Whippoorwill. Katydid, katydidn't.

My Life As an Impressionist Painting

Pay attention
                                    to the light.

The way light is always expressed through color,
because even a magic paintbrush cannot drip with light.

Light is the lemon yellow, chartreuse, grass green, and sage
                    playing in the emerald leaves. It's the silver sheen
on the fencepost and the gold spun into my hair.
                    It's the tinge of posy pink on *this* cheek, *this* arm,
this shoulder. Color is health, and light is life.

See how I am outdoors, in the long grass, near the edge of a wood.

See the gently sloping land and high, cloud-whisper sky.

                    Lower,
            at the horizon, the clouds plod along like sheep
                                    in need of shearing. Believe

that beyond my hill is another, and then another—not quite
                    so high—that dips
            into a cool river running with a music all its own.
Trout swim the river, iridescent muscled flesh
                                    propelled by bony tails,
the surface broken by dorsal fins, light tossed outward, downward
                    through the dappled water to splatter sand below.

How is this my life, you ask?

Because I've just imagined myself a fish, taking refuge
in the undulating reeds, finding delight in the water coursing over
        my supple, scaled body.

Can't you see it in my face? The way my eyes
        are half-squinted toward the farthest dreaming hill,
                my chin tilted
toward the wild abundance of the earth—
        and the other half of my vision is turned
inward,
        lungs become gills in the distant river.
Notice the way I was smiling
                just before the brush could conjure my lips.

Lament

Where were you
when the mums lost color
and the cellos bickered
and a wet wind blew? I dreamed
of a giant date,
the slender pit pulled
from the sugary flesh,
the pale close fibers

resisting. I dreamed gold
letters: my maiden name
over the window
of an old fashioned bakery.
The storefront was painted
a shiny red and cobbles
covered the street. I dreamed
and dreamed and then

I didn't. Night was a pitch
black forest you move through
like typewriter keys
but there are never any trees.
Mornings were noons
were evenings were dull.
When the night found its
way again and swam up
through the blue, I dreamed

all the tests came back
negative, and my hands grew
mottled—faint purple and
green in distinct facets,

like pottery. It was a sign,
but of what? My throat was
closing? My heart was pulled
hot from the kiln? White like
bone, it was nothing

you would cup in your hands
for comfort, evoking no
tenderness like a fallen
sparrow or a mouse
with a pulse like wishing.

Incomplete Interview with a Writer

INTERVIEWER: So. You're a writer.

WRITER: Yes.

INT: What do you write?

WRI: This and that. Mostly to do lists.

INT: Fascinating. Writing related to do lists?

WRI: Sometimes. Sometimes they're more like, buy kale and toilet paper. Look up house plants toxic to cats. Call Mom.

INT: And then you cross off each item when you complete it?

WRI: Yes. Highly satisfying. Or, if the list gets too messy, or I have too many lists, I organize and consolidate them. Also satisfying.

INT: Organize how?

WRI: Call. Buy. Do. Read. That sort of thing.

INT: What's the longest period of time something has stayed on a list?

WRI: Oh, months.

INT: What sorts of things get pushed to the next list?

WRI: Making difficult phone calls. Writing things that matter. Let's just say I've never gone without toilet paper.

INT: What's next on the list?

WRI: I'm not sure. Maybe throw the list away?

INT: But then . . . what would you do?

WRI: Stretch. Look out the window. Pay attention.

Sometimes a Sadness Comes

Why sadness, beneath the giant maple with its new leaves,
its flicker of cedar waxwings? Why sadness

in this sunlight, welcome stranger after months of gray
and cold, after weeks of rain dredging the city of itself?

When the waters came, you recalled your premonition:
sidewalks crumpled like the back of a centipede,

houses caved in like old men in hunger and without hope.
Coming out of hibernation, blinking your eyes, health

restored, fiber by fiber, cells swelling like air filled with music,
the sound of laughter in the streets, damp geraniums

pressed against the glass like a cat's firm nose—
All the world is looking

and none are paying attention. How fragile the strands
of the chrysalis, how chilling and obvious the dark forms aching

toward the light. So naked, so full of the history that ticks along
like negatives on a reel. Each image its inverse: left is

right, light is dark, and only the distant eye can perceive the whole.

And Then the Props Withdraw

From the Emily Dickinson poem beginning
"The Props assist the House"

When my father turns seventy, he begins speaking Cat.
A string of feline emojis often appear without
a texted word or phrase. The year is new
and more days than usual are sunny. Leap Day

surprises, and our eighth anniversary. I read myself
to India, Poland, Croatia, inside the brain. I finish
Emily Dickinson's selected letters. Now, every time I squint

on a sunny day, I quote inside my head, "The snow glare
offends my eyes." I wish I could show her
my giant geranium—geranium tree!—climbing
to the top of my once-a-closet library, light
hungry, a cluster of prayer plant gathered at its feet.

Coffee low in the cup, Grandma Rose's green milk glass.
She just left her home for assisted living. On the phone,
I mention the geranium, how I think I got her green thumb.
"I thought I noticed some of it was missing," she says.

The connection is poor and her voice grows tired.
And the everythingness of everything
makes finding words difficult. Our landlord is showing

the house today. Maybe we'll have to move. Eight roses
droop in a jar—yellow, red, peachy-pink. This one,
here, has unfolded most generously. *It doesn't know
you're here to give to*, I tell myself. *It's a plant: it simply* is.
On the roof next door, melting ice flashes, unexpected river.

When the Tamarack's Needles Turn Golden

Doubt
everything.
Let everything hurt.
Let memory be mouse
and bone.

In the woods,
a ravine holds a lake.
Sometimes
you hold this lake in your hands.
The lake holds
the stars. Wind—

be gentle.
Trees, listen
and be kind.
It is quiet here.
Even your breath
disappears. Some days,
snow comes home
to the water.

Words are moss.
Words are a cold
stone in the throat.
Be a fawn. Be

a rabbit,
a rabbit's breath.
Let the light
blur.

The Day Is a Too Big Jacket

Before falling asleep I decide
tomorrow I will take my anxiety on a walk.
But in the morning, frozen
rain hits the windows like
a bully throwing gravel. Okay—
so, okay. Me, the houseplants,
books and candles, fuzzy sweater
and my little pal, anxiety.

"Maybe you should stop
drinking coffee," they say.
And I think, sure, then
Anxiety can crawl onto my shoulders
like a monkey and clasp
its hands over my eyes. I could
bumble around with Anxiety
clinging to me, or I could
be alert, at least know
where it stands. Maybe

by the radiator this morning.
Anxiety likes to be comfortable.
Anxiety likes to be a deep plush
bed with white sheets warming
to your body, something difficult
to crawl out of. But Anxiety is lazy, too—
just hangs around, waits for ruts
to wriggle into, tender places of decaying

mental-emotional soil stripped
of nutrients. Here's a favorite
rut: family member dies in a car crash.

Another: random gunman enters
classroom or shoots from a car
with a noisy fan belt. Of course,
I can tell Anxiety how irrational
that is—how a couple different
car owners in a southern town
shooting guns into spring's
blossom-lined streets was an anomaly,
how the same car sound
here in dewy April doesn't mean
a bullet through the back. But of course

millions of bullets exist

in the world—and I am just lucky.
Most of us are just lucky.
No, for me, Anxiety is more like
a hairstyle you wear and wear
without seeing it's gone out of fashion.
It curls up like a Labrador
at my feet, a steady companion
that bites my toes. But really,

Anxiety is more like a note
you tune your strings to, or a sensation
in the back of your throat.
It's imaginary numbers,
and black holes, the vibration
that makes glass shatter.
In other words, Anxiety is almost

Nothing. And you can't push
Nothing out of a window or cut
Nothing into bits with kitchen shears.
Nothing you try works, except

maybe the walk. I shouldn't
divulge the whole plan here,
but it might involve a trip
to the shore where I search
for driftwood and stones and
Anxiety gets pecked to death
by sea gulls. Or maybe

a walk around the block
is all that's needed: a clean sun,
fat robins hopping through drenched grass,
the smallest branches still beaded
with rain. I'll imagine Buddha
sitting under one tree and
Jesus kneeling under another
and anxiety will forget me, distracted

by not stepping on the sidewalk cracks,

by the tremor in each puddle
approached by anonymous cars, the water
whirring up in fans of light.

Another Morning

after Suzanne Gardinier

Hot water, fresh lemon. A red coat
on a cobalt morning—not yet.

The shovel's scrape, a tilted note,
your dreaming eyes not yet

awake. Last night's laughter
smiling on the walls. Last night's

love softening the day. Music
from the accordion's bellows

breathing into the air—not yet.
A blank canvas in another room.

The painting that follows us
everywhere: squares of circles,

snails of color. Which are you?
I am the earth-water-fire.

But not yet. Your glasses on the table.
And the houseplants with their indigo

shadows, thirsty. Lemons on a tree
in Spain. Two new people speaking

a new language on a day not yet
made up. White froth curling

over and over on the forever sea.
The postcard we'll scribble out

for our shadow selves. That we'll
slip from the mailbox, surprised,

when we return on some snow blue
morning, but not yet—oh, not yet.

Words Become Strange

Maybe the wind
is harbinger, portent.
Maybe it's air
just sick of standing still.

We crisscross
lines of string
to parts of story
on a grass green rug.

At the grocery,
the clerk offers a list
of gluten-free products
organized by section.

In another part
of this world, children
are so traumatized
they've forgotten how to cry.

I check the weather,
pick out tomorrow's clothes,
wonder if the neighbors are home
it seems so quiet.

Murder in Winter

I didn't know there was a sound.
Then I could feel it, but not quite hear it.
Then I heard it, but couldn't place it.
Then it was the neighbor's trees full of crows.

Crows flying in and flapping
and scratching their black sounds
into the sky. It was the air itself, reticent.
It was darkness residing as feather-shaped
emptiness in the kitchen beside me,
nothing silently brushing my skin.

But of course: just birds, intelligent, dark
against light, invisible sound waves
and matter in motion. Sun a watery
bowl of gruel weeping from leftover
clouds. Crowds of crows like skulls
capping trees naked of leaves, frenetic
neuron scribble of energy and sound.
From where have they flown and where
will they go? Why gather here, now?

The tree's bare fingers scrabble in my gut,
darkness searching darkness.

Daily Reminders

You are driving east on Leonard.

The year is 2013.

This is the name of the town where you live.

This is your name—your age—the color of your hair.

You have been married for five years.

First came the war, then the ocean and the river.
Next the mountains, now the lake.

You have reached milestones, landmarks. But it is possible
you will not be remembered.

You have been well, and you have been ill.

You have traveled to nine countries. If you were a
cat, you would have nine lives.

It is Spring.

Yes, those great uncles and aunts really did die.
You have not, but you will.

You might be yourself again someday.

Tea is good. Love is better. You are loved.

You are still driving east on—Leonard? Yes, Leonard.

The pavement is wet.

It is afternoon.

Before After

after Louise Glück

I was granted a pair of wings to wear, invisible; shown
the door stood open and a ribbon of light streamed through.

Silence takes many forms. Many shades of darkness.
The earth damp around my body, my skin loving it, becoming it.

Memory of a chickadee streaming a ribbon of light in its beak

could not reach me. Your voice:

it brushed the capsule of air around me only,
mute and indecipherable,

forming an emptiness of itself.

Time passed, but time was immaterial: centuries, days.

Isolated from self and light and other, unable

to feel. Not even a pine bough, needles smooth
and dry, not even agony calling forth voice,

giving way to a trickle of sand, a startled spider.

And then, the light—
the semblance of day and its pale colors.

The wind forming its voice, entreating each aching
through that tunnel which is unending.

This is where spirit receives breath,
flesh remembers bone,
music and blood rush

in that deep forest no longer treacherous.

Alert to every rush of moving air, aware
of every acorn nestled in the earth, we rise golden,
scarlet, and green, enfolding all:

a holy presence casting
great salty shadows, a cloak of darting silver light.

To the Patron Saint of Ceiling Cracks

I will remind you—
moon-skinned and
owl-boned—that
you are the barren
trees' calligraphy
tossing love letters
to the sky.

Tell me again that I
am the chrysalis,
I am the fiddlehead
fern, I am the sycamore
standing naked in the rain.

5.
Even the Purple Shadows

In sleep, his hand

finds hers, holds it
warm, alive. Slight
stirring under the sheets
and sleep again.
She'd been scared
when he first returned
that he'd dream the enemy,
feel her body beside his,
and strike out.
But he never did.
He kissed her
in his sleep, told her
that he loved her.
He made a shell of his body
and scooped her in,
warming her against
the cold air traveling
through the wall, against
the troubles to come.

Communion

The way I wait
for the perfect moment
to eat my morning oatmeal—
coffee and bowl ready
at the same time and quiet
seeping into the room—draws me close
to you: sacrament of cereal
in morning's slanted light, sage
green and cream counter top marked—
I think?—with a pattern like toile,
but in the eye's brushwork, more
like the veined underside of a leaf,
like the leaf encased in the plastic
of your cereal bowl into which, regally,
you will lower the spoon. Bowl of Cheerios,
Grape-Nuts, or Wheaties, skim milk
filled to the out-curving lip.
Anyone else would spill.
Quiet as memory, I won't disturb: you just poured
the milk. Just sat on the last stool
at the counter, set down the bowl
by your tiny dish of prunes, cream with coffee.
You just took your first bite.

No Address Needed

Nothing's changed at the bar
except the fact it's never been changed
has caused the linoleum to crumble apart
in gray, mealy chunks and the red
vinyl stools to split down the middle,
sticky and scarred. This is where we go
for Grandma's 90th—Grandma, my mom,
my aunt, and me. Even the bartender
is the same, just with deeper furrows in his face,
like a cornfield plowed under. Our stools
wobble on the uneven floor like uncertain
satellites. We prop our elbows on the bar
and order up some beers.

Grandma makes the barkeep guess
how old she is today, then proudly tells him her age.
Past his ruddy face and a jumble of booze
runs a window framing a black lake fringed
with pines. For a moment the freewheeling sky
above the water is matched by a patch
at the open door as a man comes in and hefts
a leg over the stool at the end of the bar.

In their too-loud whispers, my elders
recount the days of Polish weddings
and Saturday dances, how this man used to get
so sweaty he'd step out back, peel
his shirt off, wring it out, and return
to the dance floor. Someone says hello
and they exchange the usual related to
so-and-sos down by so-and-so's and do-you-
remembers. Then Grandma (after mentioning

that she's 90 today) perks up again and says
to the man, "We used to call you sweat blossom."

We fade into something between embarrassed
silence and beer-hushed giggles. Oh, to be 90.
To be back at that crummy bar held
in the elbow of a country road miles
and miles from God knows what, tucked
in the heart of us and just exactly then.

Donuts Among the Dead

Twice now I've walked through the cemetery
with my grease-whispered bag, brown paper
crinkle O not-too-sweet dough, resisting
then soft, I'm sorry, I said, the first time.
Flash of a mirror placed over a grave. Flash
of a flicker's giveaway yellow in dangling baby
green leaves. A deceased man with the given
name Shade. Who lies in the shade. Who lies,
who truths, who knows what stories
this green acre holds. I want to write them all.
Instead I call my dad, with his cats and his taxes,
late, with the blinds just opened and flash
of orange, swift fox in the valley. I dream of foxes,
I dream of impossible things: my parents
easing the other's loneliness. In the end,
a tree that looks dead with its clutches
of closed green umbrellas. A flake of dough
and grass a hesitant question at my ankles.
What grows out of death, what questions we see
we never asked. Grass growing longer than a grave.
In the distance, a metal roof, shining like
water, shining like everything I want to believe.

Ask Me How I Know This

If you borrowed my book
and brought it back one day in the rain,
covers closed tight
to your chest and the warm pages
pressed skin-side of the zipper—

then, when the after
image of your hand
tugging the book free floats
in my mind like the petaled
hand of an old man practicing
tai chi on a hill—no, when I

remember how droplets of water
stayed shy in the drier
strands of your hair—

then, I will take up the book
and hold it close to my
closed eyes and breathe
your secret scent of pine.

I'll feel the forested dunes
rise up around me and taste lake air
laced with moss and pitch and I'll wish
for an owl but the light is just

leaving. And I'll wish for a salamander
but the earth is too dry.
For your feet
sifting soft hollows as you walk,
I will listen

the way rocks become sand.
I will eat listening the way a
shore-washed fish
gulps the cooling air. Even
the purple shadows will be listening.

You + You

I understand you. You, you
say, want to disappear. This is about

you, but when you walk
down to the shore to meet

your mirrored self, you might
bend and lift me

from the sand: an oval pebble,
wave-smoothed and flat,

slate gray and cool at first touch.
I'm quickly warmed by your hand.

You notice the little bit of rough
still left in me—you pinch me up

before the dull orange and milky sky,
note my slight asymmetry.

They say it's symmetry
that ignites the brain-light "beauty."

(What if we matched each other,
mole for mole? Would you walk

with me always, beautiful doppelganger,
made-up twin? You thought I was

stone, but ha! I have legs, warm flesh
that pinks in the sun.) But this is about

essence, and whether or not we are
ourselves. Or, speaking of symmetry,

have you seen a cypress
leaning out to sea? Theory of beauty

disproved. Watch as that pelican
glides on leathery wings, turns its head.

Listen—what song is it dreaming?
Only wind and silence. What shape

would silence hold; but then,
is silence a vessel, or held, or both?

Nothing exists in a vacuum. (Say that
both ways.) (Ways both that say.) Nothing

exists in a vacuum. A ceramic fish
can't swim and the cave of a mouth

holds no light. Curled up shadows =
words the speaker will not say.

The Meeting Place

I used to open the middle bureau drawer
and touch the jewelry resting there.
Mostly costume, some silver, more gold,
all arranged in a town of tiny mauve
apartments. Did I hold a pair of earrings
to my ears, a necklace to my throat? I don't

remember this, I don't remember thinking,
someday this will be me. I don't know
if you were present or if in stealth I opened
that other secret drawer, your drawer
filled with treasures—sacred only because
it seemed so to you, because it was packed
with bright bandanas wrapping objects
whose stories I didn't know and in a way,
preferred not knowing, better that way,
imagined; because the drawer exuded

a scent of spice, a scent of wood and clay,
a scent of forgetting and remembering, a scent
of you. Behind me, the bedspread was dark
and cool, writhing with flowers in colors of
rust, mourning dove, curdled cream.
But why am I in your bedroom? Sadness

lingered there, though it's not where it began.
It began before I crawled, frightened, between
the sheets, before your simple voice and patient hands,
before your mother and hers. It wasn't born
here or in Poland or anywhere. We all wake up
holding it, it's just a matter of how we mold it,
shape it, how it gets away. Once the hamster escaped

its cage in the family room and we couldn't
find it anywhere. We thought it had found a hole
someplace and squeezed through, or slipped

out the door when someone stepped outside.
Maybe you thought we would find it one day
by smell, after it had curled up somewhere and died.
We found it in a second floor bedroom,
imagined it crawling the carpeted stairs.
Who can say how a thing gets from one place

to another? Who can tell if it will last
once it's there? I knew what real happiness
looked like, when it was just another shade
of makeup and survival. Look, look
at the photographs, look at the gray in your
blue eyes, the mechanical pull to the corners
of your mouth. Can you really believe I lacked
the emotional intelligence to have known?
I'm part of you, remember. I don't believe
you owe me anything. But validating my experience—

accepting it, sitting still with it as if it were a fox
with a wounded leg—that would be a kindness.
That would be a white flag that folds up fighting
with pride, that would be laying it to rest in a drawer.
It can be an accessible drawer—you can open it,
smooth your hand across that flag like a prized

heirloom linen, even with affection. But please,
no unfurling. You have nothing to gain and more
to lose. I would give you a mellow day without

any worries if I could. No, a tender day on an owl's wing,
wind-ruffled and noon-still. Pine-sun, sky flung wide,
heart like a free-roving stream.
I'd say set accusation and fear on a shelf,
but there are no shelves, only limbs and leaves and
everything leaves but it's all right here.
We're alright here. A rustle in the reeds

and a thousand wings of light on the water.

Frida and Joan

I'd rather stay home and devise
an elongated fetching pole to snag
the bag stuck high in the maple
beyond the balcony. I'd rather
sit in mostly nothing with windows
wide, wait till the earnest buds
startle into leaves, watch the wind make
metamorphosis of the branches' black-ink show.
The sister-cats' ears and whiskers twitch
in their sprawl and scrunch of sleep.
I'd rather narrate their dreams
to the Everett piano and ever-obliging
jade, or collect metallic pink tinsel bits
shimmering on the rug from the cats'
dismembered toy. The possibilities:
designer bird nests, sparkle spilling
from an envelope, mixed media pieces
with fortunes from cookies like *now
is the time for action* and *you are on the brink
of great happiness*. So much happens
when nothing is happening. Cats
named for painters that labored and fought,
that felt every nuance and passion so deeply,
all color and drive and lust of every kind.
And also, they just didn't give a damn.

Good morning, my love—

I ordered you sunshine
on a big blue platter. New
artwork for the windows.
Fresh leaves on the geraniums.
I asked the notes of
Hungarian Dance #5 to slip
from the piano and keep you
company while I'm gone.

Gone is such a funny
way to say "away"—
as if we didn't understand
object permanence, and my
returning at the end of the day
was the sudden appearance
of a brand new person,
brief miracle in tired shoes.

Any number of reasons

to return. The elusive parrots
of Telegraph Hill, for starters.
The Irish coffee we never drank.
That great gasp of beauty called
Kehoe Beach, left too soon,
breathless. More books, of course.
More *I, too, could have a house*
with a lemon tree out back.
The scent of jasmine, ocean, and
ancient pine. Mornings walking
up a mountain. Baby irises,
view of the bay. The possibility
that comes with any travel, yes,
but stretches even wider when you've
left your tight-knuckled life
for a gulp of sunshine, blue bowl
tipped out across shaggy expanse.

It's the new way we feel ourselves
here and the new way we are together.
Different self + different self = new us.
You'll read the Beats and drink
zinfandel, I'll drop my headaches and my
no, this way back in winter and never
find them again. Sea lick and
light, surfer smiling for a photo,
a stuffed bear and a story
that's not quite true. Feeling small
and like this is how it should be.
A friend said the phrase,
my little life. And I took it as
sincerity frayed with falseness,

something to do with piety
and the need to stay afloat.
But little, indeed. That picture of me
among redwoods, dressed
all in black: my face a peeled walnut,
hands skeletal and over-large.
A marionette in wind song.

But there was no wind—only quiet
and stillness and rays of light
dreaming down through the ferns
patient as dinosaurs, their shadows
so unbearably full of what can't
be uttered. We try to be still, we
try, we do, but something in our hearts
keeps rushing. It urges us onward
with our cameras and our hope,
laughter and slivers of rage
lying trapped in our throats.

Remnant

She painted him love notes on pages
torn from books. When she was sick,
she watched murder mysteries on PBS
whose characters all had names no one
in real life was lucky enough to have.
When she was well, her sick self
became just another character:
in her real life, she snipped basil
and poured red wine and daydreamed
travel and night dreamed animals.
The fans whirred. The leaves swayed.
And he came back, without the notes,
from wherever her illness had banished him.

Composition

What if you split it up.

What if it was just lemon
poppy seed bread with butter,
lightly toasted, sip of coffee.
Just that.

           Then, to the compartment
on the floor, where the sun's
opening windows, turning pages.

Poems to arc and gather,
thread and weave.

What if, just this:

and later, some fish—
pan-fried—and a crisp white wine
and the light low.

Your toes touching mine
under the table.

6.
Where the Grass Still Greens

Day before Solstice, Week after Rain

At Roselle Park, the paths are paved with mud.
Here, where the grass still greens
              along the wooden bridge,
     the water has receded
                  and left in its wake
a scattering of snails—
            perhaps incapable of
     bewilderment, slow and ancient
as always, each snail traveling the same
         blade for hours, maybe days.

The quaking and shade of two
            human feet startle small
dark shapes to springing: no, not flies,
        but tiny frogs, perhaps
     intended to have hatched at the water's edge.
Angular and perfect
      as if chiseled from the very earth they resemble.

And this sound: is it the suck
of rubbery, webbed feet in the river squelch
       or the slick of snail slime
   as each muscled shell
makes the imperceptible trek toward water?
       Or some resonance of humid air
and white heat in the dense, still grass?
     Or maybe the ears of grass, listening.

Poor Oatmeal

Some mornings the flame
sends it crawling to the
saucepan's sides, where
it hardens as a crust

and I read one more
poem and sip strong
coffee that doesn't
drip into the white haze
of my mind. Self-

preservation, hormones,
or unity with the blank
winter sky—whatever

it is, I'm safe here,
and anything is possible.
Join me, if you wish, and my

lumpy pillow and faithful
pet, melancholy. Remember
the postcards you never wrote,

the pine cones tumbled
into your pocket on walks
with the dog that wasn't yours,
the scraps of words
gathered from coffee shops,
daydreams, newsprint,

and sleep. Remember
the fables and how, once,
all of them were true.

Girls at Window by Berthe Morisot (1892)

When the younger sister whispered,
it looked like she was trying to eat
the tart cherry pout of her lips without
moving. "Is this what it's like
to be grown up?" she asked.

The elder sister waited for the painter's eyes
to return to her canvas. "Of course,"
she replied. Being the elder,
it was her duty to know.

"Then I don't want to be grown up,"
the younger continued. A wisp of her fringe
tickled her temple. She squeezed
her hands tighter in her lap. "If we can't
play in the garden," she continued,
"couldn't we at least sit looking at it?"

She'd been instructed to look at her knee,
which kept trying to lift itself from the sill
and propel her leg into the garden.
And after her leg . . .

"But then she couldn't see our faces, silly,"
the elder replied. "The painting would be
awfully dull without our faces."

The younger thought it awfully dull
showing her face, especially with the lemony
September sun on her shoulders and the grass
so long and full after a summer's worth of rain.

"Don't fidget."

"I'm *not* fidgeting."

"Even Giselle is more patient than you."

The mother cat kept her eyes fixed
on the kittens curled in the elder's lap.

The elder, who was only two years older
than the younger, was wearing her best
white organdy with puffed sleeves cinched
at the elbows, a double ruffle at the hem,
and a satin sash. Her shoes pinched.

(The younger sister knew this by the way
her sister's features bunched at the center
of her face, a look like spitting, before she
caught herself and smoothed them out
the way ladies straighten impeccable skirts.
Would she tell their mother she needed new shoes?
To tell was to admit to growing up.)

"Marie?" Sophie whispered to her older sister
(for sisters must, in the end, have names).
"Do boys pose for pictures, too?"

Marie's shoulders sank down
in their organdy clouds, closer
to the windowsill's green horizon. "I suppose
they must," she whispered back,
though Sophie knew she wasn't sure it was true.

Maybe Mother was home preparing
a cherry galette. This horrible sitting
would be more bearable if only a cherry
galette waited steaming on the checkered cloth.

A thyme scented breeze sifted over the sill.
The fur above Giselle's nose glistened like the crest
of a wave in the sea that Sophie longed to visit.
Every summer, Papa tousled her hair and said,
"Perhaps next year." Somewhere in the blue

treetops (for she knew they were blue
this time of day, even though she couldn't
see them), a lark called. Giselle's eyes darted
to the shifting branches. Her pupils slimmed
to crescent moons waxing and waning together
in the gold galaxy of each eye.

"It's getting awfully warm," Sophie whispered.
The garden shimmered green on one side, the living
room sank cool and shadowed on the other.

"Just a while longer," the artist murmured.
Her voice seemed to emanate from the palette
and easel, or maybe from the items in the room,
their lilac shifting to purple and burnt sienna
drifting to umber—a voice that grew from the
contours and shapes of things themselves.

The while grew and grew till it was a shoe
filled to tight to bursting. Behind the girls,
the willow tossed its hair and a shiver

of pleasure ran through the grass.

From the corner of Sophie's eye, Marie seemed
gauzy, less real than her dress, like a breeze
might flow straight through her. Spider's web.
Cotton fluff tugged by a skirmishing wind.

"It's because you're young and pretty, with such
obedient kittens," their mother had said.

But now the artist's voice flowed out of the room
like a shaded stream: "Ah, such glorious hair.
Like burnished copper aglow."

Sophie's right leg began to swing, patent
leather shoe tap-tapping the wall.

"Only a while longer," Marie reassured her
in a voice so soft Sophie thought of a statue
you imagine has whispered in the park.

After, we'll put on our dancing shoes

while across the street, white-tailed deer
bend to eat beneath the neighbor's fir.
And stirred by the fingers of a March rain—
snow still on the ground and shrinking
into smaller and smaller bodies of white
on the Adirondack chairs—
the trees dance inside themselves, motionless.
Under their everyday colors they put on a sheen
of red, or green, or a mix of the two
that doesn't turn back to brown.

We, perhaps wishing we were trees,
are cast in the spell of seclusion, house-
sitting forty miles from home. And I know
what a waste it is to feel annoyed
by the cat's claws on my yoga mat,
by the dog trailing me and begging
even though he just ate. And of the worries,
the workload, the misplaced and
misused words, I know it's a waste
to hold any bitterness in my heart.

And the proof is where proof always is:
here, in the brief press of our hands across
the table, there in the wet branches happy
with their growing buds. It's on the couch
with the dog, snoring, in the easy
breathing of bad news temporarily delayed,
in the cat's luxurious belly
offered to the fire's heat, and in
the deer, already gone.

Ancestor Vision

When I pause in the kitchen
to fill my water glass
in a smudge of gray light,
my eye startles at the flap
of tarp on the neighbor's
firewood. *Animal!* instinct
cries, disappointment biting
the heels of fleeting belief
that motion means creature,
means bright-dark and wild
and necessarily, not entirely free.

Hand-Me-Down

I'm told a Stradivarius three hundred eight
years old is played to stay in tune, plucked
to keep its memory. Centuries, it holds,

of Tchaikovsky and Bach in countless crowds
shrouded in hush, each heart's escape inside

cadenza, the leap of ritornello. How time
hovers—suspended, yet perfectly measured.
I sit with thought and silence now on a pillow made
with my mother from salvaged cloth that didn't burn

in the farmhouse fire when she was nine.
Grandma Rose's cloth, a '30s print, I think,
perhaps once rough, now merely textured.

Red and white shapes like gardening spades
bear sprays of flowers yellow and blue.

And in my dresser drawer I've tucked
her old kerchief, its geometry of forest and dusk
thinned by time and those regimental curlers
keeping guard across her scalp on Saturday

afternoon. She parboiled the potatoes, killed
and plucked a chicken. Sunday morning,
they went to Mass, come hell or high water. It drizzled

the day we buried her. Although—
they didn't lower the casket into the ground

while we stood by, holding our roses

between two fingers. The tent dripped
on my umbrella and the grass
needed mowing. Would she have liked

this round white pumpkin gracing my table?
It glows in autumn sunlight and I want
to make more of my hands that shape

a trellised globe around its firm outer flesh.
My hands after the hands and hands that held it.

The seed, the black earth that nourished.
The everything of soil: what lives, what lived.
In the basement at Saints Peter and Paul,
near the line for kielbasa and pork and sauerkraut,

my great aunt reaches for my hand. She holds
her arm almost straight by her side, palm facing
down, blunt fingers curling strength around mine.

It's Grandma's grasp reincarnate, her grip
as strong as Grandma's at the end, when we sang

Swing Low, Sweet Chariot and *Michael,*
Row the Boat Ashore. When our voices rocked her
in the unfamiliar bed. When we gave our assurances
close to her ear and, letting go, held her hand tight.

But oh, her sister's hand in the old church basement
not then or almost but now and the same: Grandma's
hand, Grandma's hand, firm and warm and forever.

After Reading A Simple Heart

Words most recently looked up: catarrh,
pasterns, quinsy. The etymology of surrender.

I find another list in a red notebook:
susurrus, awn, arista, and the phrase
everything is right here.

After my body invited illness
to be an indefinite house guest,
I sloughed off dislike of anise,
patchouli, and chardonnay.
Now I hold them close the way
a raindrop makes light
part of itself on the window.

Another phrase, perhaps fancy
trying to make fact: *birds speak*
different languages in different
countries—even their dialects
vary by region

In the back of a store open
only on Saturdays, I discover
a shoebox of Christmas
calling cards, intricate,
smudged, one signed in 1922.
I'll find a pen with gray-brown ink,
address the cards to family,
send one to myself.

What came first: the blue flowers, or the snow?
It seems certain one will outlast the other.

Words Like Luminous and Lover

Like you, the moon
favors words such as
rumpus and corridor.
She sticks out her
tongue when happy.
(She often misplaces
the tongue's *g*
with a *q*.) Please note:
she doesn't like being
upstaged by street lamps,
no matter how quaint.
She's made special
arrangements with a
certain historic district.
On Tuesdays, for example,
they put out wrought
iron and wisteria
and she performs
a little romance.
Nothing jaw-dropping.
Just enough shimmer
to make the ferns giggle.
Though maybe it's you
who's obsessed with
the ferns, not she. She's
putting curlers in,
setting sweet rolls
to rise for morning.

Someone else's house:

their photographs, their art.

Their quirky cats and crumbs from a last
                    hurried meal.

Not my watch. Not my clock
                    ticking syncopated time.

Not my train, trundling through town,
                    its vertebrae glimpsed from this house

                              on a hill. Nobody's train,
nobody's magpie, nobody's mountains

                    circling round with their sun and snow,
their great blue shadows of moving clouds.

                    How strange it is
to be here with you: hearing you in the next room,

I expect you to reappear as someone else, or me to be
                    not me now

but myself as I was or will be.

AUTHOR'S ACKNOWLEDGMENTS

Several of the poems in this collection first appeared in the chapbook *Each Darkness Inside* (Finishing Line Press, 2019).

Chariton Review: "*Portrait of Valentine Godé-Darel* by Ferdinand Hodler (1914)," "Sometimes a Sadness Comes," and "The Year of the Cicada"

The Louisville Review: "Empty Boats"

The Other Journal: "Lukewarm Coffee at a Blue Desk in Michigan" and "Somewhere in Newfoundland"

Water~Stone Review: "A Pomegranate, or a Rhyming Couplet"

Gratitude to Brooke Harris and Priscilla Atkins for feedback on an earlier draft, and to Erick, Steven, Laura, Jenny, and Michael for input on the title.

SERIES ACKNOWLEDGEMENTS

We at Wheelbarrow Books have many people to thank without whom *Toward the Wild Abundance* would never be in your hands. We begin by thanking all those writers who submitted manuscripts to the fourth Wheelbarrow Books Prize for Poetry. We want to single out the finalists, Emily Calhoun, Ann Miller, Jacob Oet, and Heidi Seaborn, whose manuscripts moved and delighted us and which we passed on to the judge, along with Kristin Brace's, for the final selection. We thank the judge, Sarah Bagby, for her thoughtful selection of the winner and her critical comments offered earlier in this book.

Our thanks to Grace Carras, Allison Costello, Shannon McGlone, Alexis Stark, and Arzelia Williams for their careful reading of manuscripts and insightful commentary on their selections, and especially to Laurie Hollinger, assistant director at the RCAH Center for Poetry, who also read the manuscripts and provided the logistical aid and financial wizardry for this project. Sarah Teppen, a previous RCAH Center for Poetry intern, designed our Wheelbarrow Books logo, which makes us smile every time we see it.

We go on to thank Stephen Esquith, dean of the Residential College in the Arts and Humanities, who has given his continued support to the Center for Poetry and Wheelbarrow Books since their inception. As we began thinking seriously about Wheelbarrow Books, conversation with June Youatt, provost at Michigan State University, was encouraging, and MSU Press director Gabriel Dotto and assistant director/editor-in-chief Julie Loehr were eager to support the efforts of poets to continue to reach an eager audience. We cannot thank them enough for having the faith in us, and the love of literature, to collaborate on this project.

Thanks to our current editorial board, Sarah Bagby, Mark Doty, Carolyn Forché, George Ellenbogen, Thomas Lynch, and Naomi Shihab Nye, for believing Wheelbarrow Books was a worthy undertaking and lending their support and their time to our success.

Finally, to our patrons: Without your belief in the Wheelbarrow Books Poetry Series and your generous financial backing, we would still be sitting around the conference table adding up our loose change. You are making it possible for poets who have never had a book of poetry published to find an outlet for their work, something becoming harder and harder these days with so many presses discontinuing their publishing of poetry, as well as supporting the efforts of established poets to continue to reach a large and grateful audience. We name you here with great admiration and appreciation: Beth Alexander, Mary Hayden, Jean Kruger, Patricia and Robert Miller, and Brian Teppen.

WHEELBARROW BOOKS

Anita Skeen, *Series Editor*

Sarah Bagby   Carolyn Forché
Mark Doty   Thomas Lynch
George Ellenbogen   Naomi Shihab Nye

Wheelbarrow Books, established in 2016, is an imprint of the RCAH Center for Poetry at Michigan State University, published and distributed by MSU Press. The biannual Wheelbarrow Books Poetry Prize is awarded every year to one emerging poet who has not yet published a first book and to one established poet.

SERIES EDITOR: Anita Skeen, professor in the Residential College in the Arts and Humanities (RCAH) at Michigan State University, founder and past director of the RCAH Center for Poetry, director of the Creative Arts Festival at Ghost Ranch, and director of the Fall Writing Festival

The RCAH Center for Poetry opened in the fall of 2007 to encourage the reading, writing, and discussion of poetry and to create an awareness of the place and power of poetry in our everyday lives. We think about this in a number of ways, including through readings, performances, community outreach, and workshops. We believe that poetry is and should be fun, accessible, and meaningful. We are building a poetry community in the Greater Lansing area and beyond. Our undertaking of the Wheelbarrow Books Poetry Series is one of the gestures we make to aid in connecting good writers and eager readers beyond our regional boundaries. Information about the RCAH Center for Poetry at MSU can be found at http://poetry.rcah.msu.edu and also at *https://centerforpoetry.wordpress.com* and on Facebook and Twitter (@CenterForPoetry).

The mission of the Residential College in the Arts and Humanities at Michigan State University is to weave together the passion, imagination, humor, and candor of the arts and humanities to promote individual well-being and the common good. Students, faculty, and community partners in the arts and humanities have the power to focus critical attention on the public issues we face and the opportunities we have to resolve them. The arts and humanities not only give us the pleasure of living in the moment but also the wisdom to make sound judgments and good choices.

The mission, then, is to see things as they are, to hear things as others may, to tell these stories as they should be told, and to contribute to the making of a better world. The Residential College in the Arts and Humanities is built on four cornerstones: world history, art and culture, ethics, and engaged learning. Together they define an open-minded public space within which students, faculty, staff, and community partners can explore today's common problems and create shared moral visions of the future. Discover more about the Residential College in the Arts and Humanities at Michigan State at *http://rcah.msu.edu.*